Payment in Memories

Payment in Memories

Poetry of

Koon Woon

Goldfish Press

Seattle

Published by
Goldfish Press
2012 18ᵗʰ Avenue South
Seattle, WA 98144

Manufactured in the United States of America

ISBN: 0978797574
ISBN-13: 9780978797577
Library of Congress Catalog Card Number

This book is for

Laura & Ellie Priebe

Acknowledgements:

Some of these poems were first printed in these journals:

Unwound, Knock, The Peregrine Muse (online), Poetry Pacific, Walt's Corner, Three Quarks Daily (online), and in the full-length book Water Chasing Water (Kaya 2013).

CONTENTS

I've told you the fragility of my love...

I've told you of the fragility of my love,
and yet how it endures like a leaf pressed into a book,

how the pain and how inappropriately the hate,
like the Nagasake and Hiroshima bombs

left a silence whereof no man can speak...
It is this that is the fragility of my love,

Knowing my awareness is pain; I leave you in my mind
the many times I think of the silence

wherein my mother's voice should drone, but
the gentle hands released me to bed where the smell of
kerosene

from the village lamp burnt past the hour of moths
when we shut the window to village crickets,

when the tender bamboo shoots, their new fragile leaves bud
in the fragility of my love for you,

as I want to travel blind with you as far into the night
until the sun rises in Japan, and I will sail my junk

into phantom waters. Yet my love endures
like cloth flapping in the wind...

Two Persimmons Side by Side

Green was the lily pad on which sat the frog,
and crimson was the light through an orange sky…
Things will be all right, this night and other nights.
I am not the most gifted, nor am I the most favored;
yet I too want to flee into your arms enamored.
I have a twin in the metropolis, high in a tower,
Half-buried in the chatter of calculating machines –
he never looks back at the village
where his brother re-digs another ditch
and sighs at his long slender fingers
that might have caressed a violin…

Somewhere in the world, two
Persimmons sit side by side on a shelf,
Ripening quietly through quiet days.
On some day of some month, all guitars will weep,
and the persimmons' red hues will deepen and deepen.
For every brother there is a brother,
and for every persimmon there's another persimmon,
but for every boy is there a girl?
And for every girl is there a promised world?
No one knows except the crimson sky
and the red, moist persimmons…

Lychee

When a woman refuses your gifts,
She's a woman in the next tenement room,
And she knows you have nothing
Nor ever had anything to give her.
And you may be an emperor,
But the palace guards don't obey you,
And is this place a palace or a prison?
On her way to the communal toilet, she looks past you,
Her eyes vacant, registering nothing, and you ask,
"Is there a man on her mind? Or a job? Or a woman?"
And she is clothed in a coarse red shirt,
The one you gave her that once
Belonged to your brother, the lawyer –
She looks like the juicy meat of a lychee in winter,
Fetched by fast chariots from a far-away province.
She walks, never touching,
Though you've lived for so many years in adjacent rooms,
And water, when running in one room, can be heard in the
other.
Her hair blower hums a forlorn tune against
The soft murmurs of a city in sleep, in fornication.
The blower hums,
"I shall never marry; I shall never marry…"

Coming Are the Days...

Perfect weather in the onset of autumn
with maples turning three or four shades...
The luxury of a sun slanting
while the city is still tourist-heavy
with vine-ripe grapes bunching as in families
and the wine on tables telling
full and round stories.
And so I ask myself –
Will I ever go to Paris
and sit at a sidewalk café
and tune my poetry as I would a guitar?
Whatever the tune,
the earth is beginning to spin,
wheat- and apple-heavy
toward a golden harvest,

then toward winter.

Conveyor Belt

I've got to get past this logjam to
trade delusions on the common market.
I've got to chug along, to smoke and squeak
Into thousands of households.
More needed than Dutch cleanser,
more desired than perfume,
the perfect gift,
grits for kids,
even a thigh bone for the family dog.
Consumers,
I come along:
I am the Provider,
alms for a listless day,
folk remedy for a rainy afternoon.
I compact the garbage
I get you online
I remove unwanted hair
I am the solution
I am affordable
I am death on the installment plan
I am sugar
I am ashes
I am a promise
I am the choir in heaven
I will get you there.

The Odds

The odds are not good,
never were good.
Even the dishes are stacked against
me (I don't say "you")
and I have to wash them.
Eventually I will break a dish or two;
maybe a cup, or a saucer,
then, that may bring us closer, or
farther apart, to a common disaster.
You have been far away
you don't remember
when or where
anymore. You came to me
as a leaf blown.
It is all right I tell you.
I too am born of chaos
when the red opposed the blue.
But at the time I found you,
I already had learned
to look upon
my small peace
with great awe.

The Way I Had to Feel

Darkness encroaches a dead tree in the forest center
as a Samurai is surrounded by a great slaughter, and
A field of cigarette butts manifests as a Westward-bound on
the streets of San Francisco
With that Parisian air of City Lights Bookstore spanning
Columbus Street

I come home but the house is no longer existing; a light rain
assails my face; I begin to feel
I miss you and this feeling is not optional

I carry a camel on my back as I walk from one oasis ejection
to another
From one frown to the next

Even with coins I lift from a dead man's eyelids
My actions are still explainable

That is, however tenuous is our link, I love you, pretty
woman,
Though you might not believe my sincerity or that you are
pretty

And so it is your perfumed handkerchief as T.S. Eliot would
say that makes him digress

In my case buffoonery boosts my ambition way up

To infinity almost that my love is climbing for you!

This is exactly how I want to feel
And to hear tender words whispered into your ear as a very
exquisite earring I am dangling therefrom

So please do not let me dangle anymore as a hanged man
For even in death I can feel with my right side the obverse

And I can take the pain – your pain, and let's roll them into
the River Ganges

My cousin swims to escape the August heat and
She says to me, "Your speech is dense as bees, but your
writing is cursive as chicken intestines."

And if there is any truth to what she says, in my country I
love you for it is the way I feel, because it is the only way to
feel…

Between Shaves

Between shaves, I grow in years
That bears a witness to your absent hand
Stroking as you would a pale fire
On the chin of your pet

Between shaves, I have lost you
To the grottoes and grovels of the underground
Where upon which the city was built
And nameless indeed the men and women
Who powdered their cheeks after each mining accident

Should life be as complicated as this?
Kowtowing to ships that bring tissue paper
For immaculating nostrils,
Lenses of stupefied clerks, the fat cheeks of children

Between shaves, I have looked into my coffee
And known myself for the repetition of meals
And I wonder, what can I give you,
That is three-leaved and not a clover,
And will startle you into magic!

The magic of a palm and a vulnerable face between shaves
An endless stream of bills and invoices

Telling me what I should be and to live
If only to satisfy those obligations
As I flee from pillow to pillow
With clasping hands but no supporting arms
With feet sinking into sand
Touching the rims of sand dollars

And you, the daughter I did not have
And you have a mother
She never has left you
She stayed and walked these sands of the Oregon coast
The prints are gone, but it was, it was in Oregon.

The thunderous applause of oceans

(from the collection, The Way I Had To Live)

We do not say our destination is near
Or that our journey is far,
But we do know our intent wins the applause
Of oceans.

We do not say our love melts butter
Or dissolves gold,
But we know its core is the white flame
Of fire.

We do not say our companionship is for
What hours,
Nor do we say we agree or disagree,
But we know that it has been a quarter of a century.

We have to live.
We have to live this way.
We have blemishes
And so are we to blame?

You have circled the city in your car,
Looking for a place to get good cucumbers,
But the loneliness drives you on,
Of this club you are a member.

I have rattled the typewriter and the sound
Bounces and rebound in my sparse
Rented room.
I seldom see a friend or even a foe.

Now we say we have to live
Simply because
We have to live the way we do, as victims
Of secret and nameless wars.

And we live like we do,
Until we can stroll along the seashore
And to hear the thunderous roars
Of ocean and ocean waves,
Until the oceans do not begrudge us anymore.
They give us their shores
As we embrace on the sand and the waves forever applaud.

April 11, 2012

She was a strange lady; she said
the truth is calculable but I am so sad.
I was attracted to her false eye,
in the coffeehouse when I read
a philosophy text and vastly enjoyed
my coffee stirred with honey
that being young and impressionable,
I fed copious info to my head.

She studied Chaucer and the cups and saucers
of the busy café and said, " I must go to bed.
I worked on a chemistry problem and I am balancing
the valences in my head."
In the end it was no good.
The chess competition was extremely bad
although the steam from my coffee
held its own for a while

against the fog on the stained-glass window,
and outside, the snow fell. Sort of sad.

She told me of the phone company
where she patched calls
with signals coming from the other side of the world
crisscrossing in her ears.
So many people talking still, she said,
the world must still be undead.

I touched softly her hand and bid to go.
She sighed weakly as gentle as the falling snow.
In the short interlude while I touched her hand,
a lifetime slid by and henceforth
all chance meetings follow this paradigm,
as the global swelling of the earth's tides,
and our parting did not signify a good-bye...

Like Water

Today I feel like the saddest water
going to places men reject

Like water I ebb my way
to the lowest point in the dungeon

I harden myself like ice
and crack only under sufficient pressure

What about the steam power that I
once was, driving great turbines?

What about the gentle rain that I
was - lovers abed drowsed in?

What has come to pass are
transformations difficult to accept

All that hails from up above
hit the hard ground

Eventually everything is ice-capped
or ocean-bound

Lines written on my return trip from my first Pacific University MFA residency in Seaside, Oregon

I expected rivers
Instead, I saw yellowed pastures
horses standing next to junked cars

I was empty
Bought a Diet Pepsi on the train
chewed the ice

Today is like
any other after all
there were no rivers

Brown grasses
frost on the brush
along the rails taking me home

I expected assurance
but the ride in darkness
rattled me

I was empty
Bought another can of Diet Pepsi
I did not object to its price
I deduce I am the alien
the horror movies insinuate
I think I am the intruder

Into these woods
Where the January frost
cannot do much good.

Hotel Fire

When a pretty woman cries to me
like a hotel on fire
I am almost normal in response
Bring out the meat
Bring the drinks
Be merry!

Let not the fire and light go to waste!
Bring the pen
Write it down for posterity!

Jaroslav Seifert you are so right,
women do us the least harm

A lesser mortal am I
but we are all mortals alike

When a single woman cries,
the whole night is on fire!

When the hotel burns,
I quickly learn,
how quickly you arouse desir

I See My Fate in My Palm

I see my fate in my palm,
the palm that holds your palm,
and the lines and veins that connect
my heart to your heart
in the paths of life.

Be it simple, be it convoluted,
be it properly clothed, or complete in the nude,
you are my life, my fate,
you are my wife, my mate.

When men compare wallets against wallets,
or the number of hairs standing in their heads,
I compare the stars that shine each to each,
and count the days our love grows, from the day we first met.

I will not forget you in my village tongue,
by your name Lian Ai, the beautiful lotus,
and as you lie silently here asleep,
I pause at the typewriter,
to look at the lines you etched indelibly in my palms.

I see my fate, I see the paths of our connecting veins.
I can see the future too, it is always the first day –

You are my life, my fate;
You are my wife, my mate

poem of streets in the fall

Today I really got the general drift
of what the wind-blown leaves trace;
brown and manila colored, sized from
fingernails to half a palm
whirling on the sidewalk.

Wind got me too, its velocity the tepid
sun did not help, cold drafts
from the south, and it is my autumn,
sad sirens of October.
Winter the only inevitable season
bringing rain and ice to Seattle.

Today I had walked about the refurbished
parts of the city, feeling the streets
as under-brushes, the cafes and taverns
almost downbeat and sparsely occupied.

It seemed the human commerce at these
corners and parks of the city is as fast
as a handshake, a blurred scene from the
perspective of a passenger on the bus.
Going while pigeons flocked together
in the square and dispersed.

However Deep the Night, I Expect Morning

Fog rolls into the valley, rolls
Where my mind goes into the evening,
As the rhythm of city syncopates my walk,
The roar of jets, the whisper of beggars,
Parks have their statues

In this city I know
Know where to find the best soup,
Where often the bands play the pigeons flock
Above heads of idols and unknown heroes
Not far from my tenement above Stockton and Vallejo;
I play Go from a book.

Rinds of light and rain fall silently
Equally on door knobs of silver or copper
This town dreams are altered by Andy and Val
Fight domestic while mice noisily cum
They do not expect morning

I think of crimson electric when morning sun rises
Arriving like a Chagall painting
A man floats up to kiss a woman from the Bolshoi Ballet

I am writing to you as I do, ever so remorseful
The window sill announces there is rain outside
But your purring has begun here in pulses of 8 to 80
As you break night once more and again
I write to you as I do and writing as you yourself do

On onion skin the lightest of verse
The lightest of verse, the lightest of verse

.